T0209243

The Caterpillar Gets Its Wings

H. P. FOLK

ARCHWAY
PUBLISHING

Archway Publishing books may be ordered
through booksellers or by contacting:

Archway Publishing
1663 Liberty Drive
Bloomington, IN 47403
www.archwaypublishing.com
844-669-3957

ISBN: 978-1-6657-4013-5 (sc)
ISBN: 978-1-6657-4015-9 (hc)
ISBN: 978-1-6657-4014-2 (e)

Library of Congress Control Number: 2023904319

Print information available on the last page.

Archway Publishing rev. date: 04/13/2023

CONTENTS

Part II

Part III

DEDICATION

To Mami, Papi, and Abuela

ACKNOWLEDGEMENTS

I'd like to extend my deepest thank you and gratitude to the following people:

My mom for always being there for me. My dad, who, although not physically here anymore, is always with me. My abuela, my other guardian angel, for being the strongest woman I've ever known.

All of my closest friends, who were among the first to know about my secret project, especially the Core Four, Tamara, and Marsha. Thank you for all of your encouragement in writing this book and helping me to believe I could do it.

The entire team at Archway, for all of their help, hard work and guidance in making this book a reality, a physical piece of my soul out in the world to read.

Nolen, for the initial inspiration and spark to publish my poems. I'm forever grateful to you.

The universe, God, and my ancestors for leading me in ways, big and small, to this moment in time. I, thank you, truly and deeply.

And to you, dearest reader, for picking up this book. I hope at least one of these poems speaks to you and helps you on your journey.

PART I

CATERPILLAR

Hungry caterpillar,
Eager to indulge,
Savor every bite.
Drink up this world.

Moving from leaf to leaf,
Tasting all in your path,
That which nourishes your body
And that which tries to poison you.

Munching on everything
Until it becomes part of you,
Until you've taken in so much
You can no longer feast

But instead must take a reprieve.
Rest from this world.
Break free from it.
Cocoon yourself away.

FALL

A time unlike any other
When plenty turns to scarcity,
The full bloom of life
Becomes a slow decline.

The rich harvest gives way
To an unrelenting cold.
A dance between two worlds,
Life hanging between more and less.

Something turning to nothing,
Ripeness turning to ash
In the fall of your life,
Leading to the coldest winter ever.

FRIDAY NIGHT

No new messages.
Not a single one.
Your new normal.

Before this silence
Your phone chimed
All day, every day.

Messages from friends,
Sexy texts from lovers,
Check-ins from family,
And now barely a beep.
No new messages.
Not from anyone.

The silence from the phone
Loud as a sonic boom
Breaking your mind's barrier.

It explodes each time
Your eyes meet your phone
And a blank screen stares back.

Staring back at you.
Nothing to say.
Nothing to offer.

Leaving you empty,
Unseen and unheard,
An ignored speck.

WHAT IF?

What if I stay?
What if I go?
What if it works?
What if it fails?

What if we lived in the moment?
What if we lived in the present?

What if we smelled the roses?
Breathed in the fresh air?
Loved fearlessly?
Worked passionately?
Cared for ourselves?

What if we did all we've longed to do?
Took that adventure?
Moved to that place?

What if we loved the ones who loved us?
Told them we loved them?
Appreciated everything they did?

What if we lived life
Each and every day
To its fullest potential?

What if?

CHASM

The distance between two points

Too enormous to walk, jump, or leap.

Two points that cannot come together

Without some bridge to join them.

The vastness below,
A depth that echoes so loud
It reaches out of its darkness
To the surface above.
Waiting to be heard;
Waiting to be seen.

Aching to come together;
Aching to find a link.
To keep the chasm
From growing larger
Before the two sides
Can never come together.

CONNECTION

Can I get a connection?
Can I get that feeling?
That energy just right
Between two souls

Where the space closes in,
Joining them together
With an ease unseen,
An effort as light as a feather.

Until the two become one,
Each whole and complete alone
But stronger with a connection
Like neither has felt before.

TEARS

So many kinds of tears
Spilled from the heart.
Angry and happy,
Unable to tell them apart.

Pieces of your soul
Running down your face,
Trails of water
Marking their place

As you cleanse yourself
From all that you've held in,
Every moment, touch, and feeling
Pouring out from within.

So many tears shed
From emotions you thought had fled

But instead,
Took hold of your soul
And released from you,
Making you whole.

Tears help to process it all
As they trail down cheeks
That were never ready
To see them fall.

A WEIGHT

Frustrated with life.
Pissed at being second-guessed.
Annoyed at constant changes.
Struggling to keep up with demands.

Not one to pester or complain,
Head down, I do as I'm told
Because each time I try to fight,
I get batted down and smacked.
It is enough to make me scream.

The feelings become frequent.
I find myself restless, prone to anger,
Less willing to listen, eager to react.
I become unyielding and unbending,
Fixed like my star sign.

I linger in that frustration,
Let it sit on my chest,
Heavy as a weight,
Till I force it off,
Heave its great mass aside.

DESPERATION

That feeling that you have
When you want something so bad
You can almost taste it.
The feeling that comes,
Knowing you would do anything
To keep what is already yours.
That feeling that creeps in,
Whispering to you in the dark.
If you lose one thing,
Your world will come undone.

It's hopelessness.
It's despair.
It's wanting.

You want something so urgently,
Every person who crosses your path
Can smell it wafting off you,
The pungent odor of desperation.

You will do anything for it
And anything to keep it.
Keep it just for you.
Nothing else matters.

Whether giving up life's joys
Or trying to escape all of life's woes
To acquire that one thing
That will give life meaning,
Losing yourself piece by piece.
That is how desperation takes hold
And never, ever lets go.

REJECTION

Rejection hurts.
Rejection lingers.

Because we need to belong.
Because we must be connected.

Rejection takes that away;
Isolation and fear take over,
Making us feel as though
We will never belong again.

Funny how this emotion
Can make us forget
All the times we partook,
All the times we belonged.

It only remembers the hurt,
The times "no" hit our face,
When the worst in ourselves
Was the only thing we saw.

CLOAK OF DEPRESSION

An invisible cloak,
Ever-present shadow.
It never leaves your side
As you carry it day to day.

You shoulder its burden,
The heavy weight it places
On mind, body, and soul,
Its pressure all you've ever known.

Your thoughts are not your own,
Having never had freedom to grow.
Each cloaked in the shadow,
Never allowing light to show.

It seeps into your everyday
And invades in every way.
The mess you can never seem to clean.
Projects and ambitions that never come to be.
Food sought only for its comfort,
Trying to cancel every hurt.

Feeling listless and lazy.
Thoughts foggy and hazy.
It drags you down
In the tiniest of ways.

Walking through its fog,
Usually thick and dense,
Only occasionally light,
But never ever clear.
Its omnipresence
Keeping hope out of sight.

Depression lingers in the body,
Weighs on the soul,
And clouds the mind
At every opportunity.

GRIEF: AT FIRST

The kind we see
On our TV screens,
Falling to our knees
Crying, screaming out of need.

Grief at first is no easy path.
It's almost as if you are filled
With nothing but wrath,
As though you had been killed,

As if your soul were no longer here,
As if you had simply disappeared.

It takes many forms in the early days.
At first, you may cry;
You might even pray
To take all the hurt and pain away.

A pain you never knew before,
One that consumed your body and soul.
The death of a loved one,
The likes of whom will never be seen again.

With their death,
A piece of us dies,
But that piece has nowhere to go.
Unlike the soul, which leaves the flesh,
That piece stays deep in our chest.

Our hearts heavy,
Trudging forward through the storm of emotions,
Trying to make sense of all that has happened.

Some days are easy
And some days … are hard.

At first.

SUFFOCATED

Unable to breathe,
Nowhere to move,
Gasping for breath,
Trying to struggle free
To get an inch,
Just one inhale
Of precious air.

NUMB

A feeling I know too well,
A strange sensation at first.
You almost cannot tell
When the dullness sets in.

Something has changed within,
Making a home in your chest.
The emptiness settles in.
You wonder why you never feel your best.

It stays
And stays
And stays.
It never strays.

A feeling you can't shake off.
This overwhelm inhabits you;
It clings and never comes off,
Changing the very essence of you.

INVISIBLE

I might as well be a specter
For all the attention I get.

No acknowledgment
Nor love.

As transparent as Griffin in Iping
Meandering through people,
Waiting to be noticed,
Looking for anyone to see me.

Seeking anything that will
Acknowledge my existence.
That I am here;
That I matter.

Instead, so many pass by
Day after day
Never noticing
The seemingly invisible.

CENTER STAGE

Life's sorrows take center stage,
Its black tutu fluffed,
Ready for the spotlight,
Set to spin its never-ending tale.

It jetés,
Pirouettes,
Chassés,
And glissés.

Each turn and leap
Spinning life's worst moments
Into a Balanchine masterpiece
Beyond riveting to watch.

The ballet continues
Weaving your dark tale
Through the fluid movements
Of its prima ballerina.

A continuous loop
Gracefully performed,
Spotlight on the prima
As she performs flawlessly,

Displaying each heartache,
Each painful moment,
Every rejection,
And every hurt,
Leaving only the worst
For your eyes to feast on.

No room for life's joys
To have a chance at center stage.

STORM CLOUDS

The storm clouds roll in,
Bringing with them
Rain, wind, lightning, and thunder.

The rain beats down,
Drowning the land,
Soaking everything in its path.

Wind howls in the air,
Uprooting the oldest trees,
Thrashing waves against the shore.

Lightning flashes bright,
Illuminating the deep gray sky.
It strikes, scorching the land.

Thunder roars above,
The undeniable sound of a tempest
Resonating through your body.

You stand on the open field
In the middle of the storm,
Waiting for it to consume you,

Lift you away,
Carrying you
To a distant land

Free from trouble
And all you have bared so far.
Desperate freedom sought.

NATURE

In both beauty and wrath,
Nature has no equal.

From the bluest skies
To thunderous clouds,

From cool, calm breezes
To devastating tornadoes,

From gentle ocean waves
To the fiercest tsunamis,

From the mightiest oaks
To grains of sand,

Inhale its beauty,
The majesty of its colors
Splashed across landscapes,
Filling morning sky and starlit night.

Awe at its wrath,
The reach of its destruction,
Clearing out the old,
Making way for new growth.

WOUNDS

Gaping and open,
Festering and bleeding,
Oozing from every inch of skin.

Formed by life,
A mark of battles—
Those you have lost,
The ones you were unprepared for,
The ones you had prepared for all your life,
The ones you fought on another's behalf.

Though some seemingly won
The price of "victory"
Seen all over your skin,

And some wounds
Never rise to the surface,
Stay buried beneath.

The worst kind
Never seeing the light of day,
Their existence unknown to you.

OVERCAST

Gray clouds hang overhead,
Stitched to the sky
By thin lines of white
Marbling the horizon.

Its presence, a gray shadow
Blocking golden rays from above.
A hazy spirit dampening the mood,
Clouds hovering over each soul.

MOTEL ROOM

A tiny, dim space.
Cheap old bedding.
Then a knock at the door.

He enters slowly.
A sly grin spreads
From cheek to cheek.

He takes your hand,
Guides you slowly to bed,
Smiling even more.

You lay back slowly,
Your womanhood spread,
Bosom laid bare.

Flesh pressing together.
Bodies moving in rhythmic pace,
Climax slowly building.

As the night presses on,
A feeling blooms within.
An aching floods your chest.

You strive to hold it tight—
The only way you know—
A surge of constant pleasure.

You chase that feeling.
One motel room to another;
Stranger after stranger.

Confusing each with romance,
The man of your dreams,
The love of a lifetime.

You become forlorn,
Disappointed with each encounter
As you are never able to catch
That which you truly seek:

That special connection—
A partner who sees you.
A love like no other.

KIDDIE RIDE

A small choo choo
Chugging along slowly,
Bearing its tiny riders
To no destination at all.

It continues in circles,
Round and round
With nowhere to go.
Safety is its ultimate goal.

No thrills or chills,
Only the calm chug,
Steady and even,
Lulling you to sleep.

You wake still on the train
Yet no longer a child.
And despite your age,
You seem to still fit.

A wondrous surprise
Or a grim warning
That the "fine" grownup
Is nothing more
Than a child in adult clothing?

Never healing from the past,
Stuck on the small train
And its safe passages
For most of their life.

PART II

CHRYSALIS

Cocooning yourself from it all.
Resting after much indulgence.

As you hide away from the world,
You start to reflect,
To use all that you have eaten—
The good and the bad.

Your journey through taste
Has led you here;

To a season of loneliness
Where only you can discover the truth.
To use all you have taken in
And transform into something more.

WINTER

Life has retracted.
Nothing grows.
All is stagnant,
Ready for hibernation.

The cold has set in.
It blankets all of you.
The dream of solitude
Begins to descend.

Encased by the unforgiving cold,
It forces resilience from you
To cling to the warmth.
Your only way to survive
The unrelenting chill
That never gives way.

IN TIME

They say everything comes in time.
Everything you want;
Everything you need.

They say patience is a virtue.
Patience is necessary;
Patience is everything.

They say it will all make sense in time.
All the joy;
All the pain.

In time you will understand.
Understand every loss;
Understand every victory.

Right now is unclear.
Riddled with questions;
Riddled with choices.

Paths lay before us.
Paths we see clearly
And others hidden from view.

But whatever path
You choose to follow,
All will become clear
In time.

ALL THE THINGS I WANT
TO SAY TO YOU

Wish I could say how hurt I truly am.

How I wanted more than what we had.

That I feel rejected.

That I felt used sometimes.

That I think about what could've been.

That I'm jealous we didn't have what you and she have.

That I know I can't call you when I have a lousy day.

That you're no longer my shoulder to cry on.

That I feel alone.

That my heart is broken.

That I wish I was more confident.

That I feel like I've been discarded.

That the way I feel is not your fault.

That I want you in my life more.

That I'm holding on because I finally found someone worth
holding onto.

That I love you in that way.
That I know things won't be the same.
That in the end, we will be okay.
That I will be okay with time.
That you and I were meant to meet but maybe not meant to be.

How I wish I could say all these things without judging myself
Nor feel as though I'm being judged.

So I write them to help ease my pain,
To remind myself that I am loved,
Can be loved,
And will be loved.

COMFORT

I've sought comfort
In all forms.
You name it,
I have used it.
Food, sex, drink,
The list goes on.

I have relished in these comforts.
I have felt empty without them.
I have used them time and again.

And each time
They only left me feeling less.
Bits of soul lost each time.

All for the temporary fix;
The Band-Aid over the bullet wound.
Comfort to a soul in need of healing.

STUCK

In the middle.
In a holding pattern.
In a life
You did not create.

But one you stumbled into;
One that has comfort.
No risk and little reward,
Its only prize is its comfort.

There is little movement.
Up, down, backward, forward.
Seemingly no way out of comfort,
Out of ease,
Out of sustained boredom.

How, then, to become unstuck?
How to change your trajectory?
What force will it take
To change this life?

A great external force?
A burning internal force?
Maybe both
To rocket you out of this life.

Into a richer life;
A more rewarding life.
A life with purpose;
A life fulfilled.

BONE-TIRED

Your eyes close on their own.
They flutter open as you try to stay awake.
Something escapes your mouth, a low moan
Indicating each and every ache,
Coming from the depths of your being.
You are bone-tired.

A tired you feel so deeply,
It takes over your whole body.
Head bobs forward
Only to be snapped awake quickly.
Eyes continue to flutter.
Body slumps to one side anywhere you sit,
Longing for a reprieve
From this prolonged state of tired.

Tired from life;
Tired from living life.
Tired from the sleepless nights.
Tired from the worry.
Tired from the stress.
Tired from it all.

Your body knows what is necessary
For the tired and aches to leave:
Rest, glorious rest.
Deep, deep sleep,
Where dreams dare not enter.

As your muscles heal.
As your body heals.
As your mind heals.
As your whole being heals.

Heals from all it has to do.
To endure for so long.
Rest is the only way forward.
For without rest,
There is no life.

GRIEF: IN THE MIDDLE

After the funeral,
And everyone has paid their respects.
When they've all gone home
To mourn with their loved ones.

There you remain,
Possibly alone.
Possibly with your own loved ones,
Stumbling alone or together through grief.

Weeks pass by in a flash,
But the days are slow as molasses.

And suddenly it is months later,
After the funeral.

You've staggered through days.
Tossed and turned through the nights.
Pressed forward.
Stood still.
Moved backward.
Spun in every direction possible.

You've cried but less than those first days and weeks.
You've felt numb, not knowing which emotion to embrace.
You've felt every emotion at once.
Sometimes it was too much to bear,
Unsure of which mask each day to wear.

A roller coaster of emotions.
And now, it seems, the ride has slowed.
The twists and turns not as frightening;
The highs and lows not so drastic.
You can almost anticipate it.
See the emotions as they come.

But you are not overwhelmed.
You've started slowly to embrace them,
Leaned into the crying, sorrow, heartache.

Knowing how they move through you now—
Awareness of them—a sure sign of healing,
Of what it means to remember.
And at long last … you smile.

THAT GRAY FEELING

I will never forget
That day long ago,
Our professor asked,
"What color is the law?"
And in resounding unison,
We answered, "Gray."

It was the first time
That gray was something
Other than a color.

As years have passed,
Gray has become more.
Not just a favorite color,

But a way to feel.
A casual emotion,
Numb and indifferent.

Swaying from dove gray: the lightest indifference.
To deep heather gray: just shy of depression.

I live in shades of gray,
Seesawing back and forth.
Never touching bright white: overarching happiness and light.
Neither feeling deepest black: the nadir of depression.

Each morning spent deciding
Which shade to dawn that day.
Whether I will feel or not.
Whether to be half dead and numb
Or slightly alive and indifferent.
But always in that gray feeling.

BROKEN

Unmade by decisions.
Undone by choice.
Shattered to pieces
By forces, external and internal.

Each wrong turn taken
Forged a path in a wood.
One inhabited by only the worst;
The best scattered to the wind.

A gaping wound
That never heals,
Only worsens with time.
An endless torment.

THE RAIN

I used to hate the rain.
I thought it dreary,
Reminiscent of pain,
Making you weary.

Frowned at the gray clouds
Covering every inch of sky.
Storm clouds approaching proud,
Sunshine lying deep behind.

It took long to realize
The rain's true purpose.

Providing a needed break,
Washing away the pain.
The steady beat of its drops
Clearing away all mistakes.

NOISE

People having conversations,
Talking on cell phones.
Small, intimate talk;
Loud kaffeeklatsches.

All the voices and sounds
Rise and rise,
Becoming a cacophony,
Blending and distorting into one.

My ears ache from the noise.
I mentally press hands over ears,
Straining to keep it all out,
Closing my eyes against the voices.

I grab headphones,
Use them as a shield,
Blasting music at highest volume.
Anything to drown it all out.

Music brings waves of calm,
Taking front seat to all other sounds,
Providing a brief respite
From all the noise.

ANTICIPATION

The deep breath
Before the plunge.

The calm
Before the storm.

The quiet
Before the rush.

Your heart racing
As time draws closer.
It goes slower and slower,
Inching to what you've been waiting for.

One final deep breath
Before it begins.

WITHDRAWAL

I shake from the withdrawal,
A cold sweat over my body.
Head throbbing, body aching,
Itching for my drug of choice.

The need for just another hit.
One more high to feel good.
Float away on its rush;
Lose myself in the euphoria.

THE WELL-TRAVELED ROAD

"Two roads diverged in a wood, and I—
I took the one less traveled by,
And that has made all the difference[1]."

Robert Frost's legendary lines,
Sticking out like a billboard
Emblazoned on my occipital lobe.

My frontal lobe ignores those lines
And steers us clear in the other direction
That which it thought best for us.

Venturing down this well-traveled road,
Its tree-lined path offering shade,
Disguising the hidden dangers.

Distractions dot the road.
Television, social media, movies
Dulling the senses.

---

[1] Frost, Robert, 1916. "The Road Not Taken." in *Mountain Interval.*
New York: Henry Holt & Company.

Well-groomed and maintained;
Orderly and perfect.
No adventure nor risk in sight.

The path straight and clear,
No twist nor turn nor obstacle.
So well-traveled, no map is needed.

The way paved by countless before,
No need to venture off or explore.
Nothing new to see or do.

You follow it blindly,
Like so many before,
Never daring anything more.

Its rhythmic monotony
Driving you slowly insane,
Begging you to leave
This well-traveled path,
To seek new adventure
Down the other road.

GROWING PAINS

Not your typical kind,
The teenage angst
And mood swings.

Real growth
From deep within,
Down in your soul.

The kind that comes
After years of hiding
Your true self from you.

When you rethink
All you learned,
All you were taught,

You start to truly feel
For the first time in life.
Every buried emotion,
Unearthed like treasure
Ready to be discovered
And put on display

After years of being buried
And hidden far, far away.

YET TO STIR

Maya Angelou wrote
Words of great note.
"I rise."
"But still, like dust, I'll rise.[2]"

Speaking hope into life.
Out of misery and strife,
Giving the powerless power,
Those locked out the ivory tower.

But what of those who've yet to stir,
Still waiting to be heard?
Hiding away their gifted heart;
Too afraid to even start.

Heads bowed ever so low,
Seeing nothing beyond their toes.
Blinders over each eye,
Never daring to raise them high.

[2] Angelou, Maya, 1978. "Still I Rise" in And Still I Rise: A Book of Poems. New York: Random House.

The self-inflicted chains you bear,
Leaving you never wanting to dare.
Afraid of the power you hold within,
To share with the world as kin.

To those who feel this way,
I have only this to say:
If you stay in your box
Afraid to turn the lock,
In that box you shall remain,
Though you have no reason to stay.

AMUSEMENT PARK

Brightly lit signs hang overhead.
Colorful displays of adventure
Waiting for you to seize the day.

You may start out
Riding in teacups,
Spinning in place
Until they slow to a stop.
Not enough adventure
This time around.

Your next stop:
The pirate ship.
Swaying to and fro,
Giving some control.
But no forward motion,
Only making a groove,
Swaying in the same space.

The map leads you next
To a park staple:
The rollercoaster ride.
High in the sky,
You plunge down.
It twists left
And then right.
Up and down.
The epitome of thrill.
Once it stops,
You disembark,
Feeling excited
But not satisfied.

Your next stop:
Straight to Catapult Bungee.
Seeking more adventure,
Anything to fly away.
But it only pulls you back,
Knocking the air out,
Preventing any escape.

Finally, back on the ground level.
You seek less adventure,
Needing time to breathe.
A reprieve from daredevil rides.

A soothing ride along,
Where the story comes alive
Right before your eyes.
As you sit and enjoy,
Scenes of your life
Pass in color before you.
Each happy moment,
And every sharp pain.
Each muscle begs to leave,
But the mind has a plan.

Instead you wait, patiently
Reliving the moments,
Understanding each hurt,
Embracing each joy.
As it comes to an end
You are left outside the park.
Having seen the journey so far,
You eagerly embrace the next ride.

YOUR SKIN

Ill-fitting and loose,
Hanging by threads never tightened,
Not made to fit your frame.

It becomes looser over time,
Barely hanging on.
Waiting to fall off.

In time, it does just that.
Shedding itself completely;
Revealing the truth beneath.

You were never skin
Or muscle or bones.
You are a forest.

Mighty oak trees,
Your center and core.
Its strength your spine.

Fragrant wildflowers,
Their stems and petals;
Your blood and veins.

Your body is the forest,
Regenerating each time
From decay and frost.

You are all that grows.
Returning over and over,
No matter the destruction.

SHIFTING SANDS

As I begin my trek,
The sand beneath my feet
Changes with each step,
Never the same as before.

I strain to keep in step,
Trying to remember
The path I took
That brought me here.

The shifting sands
Force me to change,
To keep their pace
As the smallest gust
Keeps the path hidden,
Just out of sight.

I hasten to catch up,
Struggling to find the way.
Change becomes the norm
On these desert plains,
For little remains the same
On these vast dunes.

PART III

WINGS

Emerging slowly
From your season of loneliness,

You discover you are more—
More than when you started;
More than when you hid away.

Everything before,
Shaping who you are now.

Each and every action,
Each and every word,
Steering you here—

To a season of freedom
Where your wings were made to fly.

To carry you off
Into your colorful future.

SPRING

The king of all seasons.
Life beginning anew,
Shaking off winter's cold;
No longer clinging to the frost.

Bursting forth from deep sleep.
Rejuvenated from hibernation.
Seeking out light
After the depths of darkness.

You emerge from the winter of life.
You revive under spring's blossom.

UNEXPECTED

You came into my life
Completely unexpected.
Unlike the ones before,
So different, and yet so familiar.

You came at a time
When I was unsure.
Unsure of my next move;
Unsure of where to land next.

You saw me,
All the different parts.
The parts I let be seen,
And the parts I hid
From others
And from myself.

Our meeting was of two ships passing in the night.
Two souls with a deep connection
And a sparking chemistry.

A chemistry I wanted to last,
Wanted to hold onto for as long as I could.
A chemistry that made me feel
Alive in a new way.
A chemistry that sparked in me
A new phase of life.

So for as long as I live,
Wherever I go and whoever crosses my path,
I will always think of you.
For you helped me to this new road.

You were unexpected.
And for you, I am forever grateful.

ROOTS

The thing about roots is,
You don't see them.

Plant roots,
Tree roots,
Family roots.
But they are ever present.

Beneath the surface,
Anchoring you to the ground.
Providing security when it feels none exists.
Giving a foothold in an unsafe world.

Sometimes you can feel your roots,
Connect to them,
Channel them,
Feel them guide you upward.

Sometimes you've grown so high
You no longer feel them,
No longer connect to them,
No longer see how deep they go.

Until water is scarce,
Until resources dry up,
Until you need them to dig deep,
To find new resources,
To find you nourishment,
So that you may grow again.

And in this next growth
You will be stronger,
All because of your roots.

REST

A simple four letter word
Meaning to cease work or movement,
A period of relaxation,
An object not in motion.

Momentum stopped,
Work ceased,
Life paused
So that one can simply exist.

A fundamental part of living
So often ignored.
"I'll sleep when I'm dead," they say.
"YOLO," shouted by the masses.

Not hearing above the noise
To find that tiny part of you
Longing to be still,
To stop and rest.

We are not meant to go on forever
Without rest.
We are not machines,
We are souls—beings
Meant for more than productivity.
Meant for more than output.

Life cannot continue without rest,
Without laying down,
Without pausing,
Without reflecting.

To give pause and choose a direction;
See where life has led thus far
And the many places we will go
On a journey that will take us near and far.

We have divine purpose
From the universe,
Or whichever deity you choose,
To lead full lives
Filled with breaks and pauses,
Mixed with the bustling activity
That makes up all life.

To pause the endless stream
And live in the moment.
Be still with ourselves
And listen to the universe
Shouting at us
To be at rest.

LINGER

Do you think of me from time to time,
Or am I always on your mind?
Does the scent of me linger
On the tip of each of your fingers?

Do you feel me on your skin?
Does it make you rise from within?
Does your blood rush,
As a moan comes forth from touch?

Fingers hovering, desperate to serve,
As strong hands caress unending curves.
Softest pillow lips kissing mine.
Passion overflowing and ever divine.

Hands gliding on silky flesh.
Soft bosom pressed to rippled chest.
A whisper of breath
Arouses every hair on the neck.

Ever a cunning linguist,
Lips linger before the first kiss.
Hands pressed on smooth thighs,
Ecstasy flowing from where fingers lie.

Blooming like a rosebud
Peaking before the flood,
The rise coming from love.
Ecstasy brought from the flick of a tongue.

Hands gripping skin
As you pull yourself within.
Hip to hip, a gentle thrust;
Bodies intertwined by lust.

A night to never forget.
Passion neither would ever regret.

GRIEF: FOREVER

No longer a rollercoaster ride
But rather a maze.

Most days you can find your way,
No longer lost in the bushes,
Meandering to find a path.
But there are days you feel lost:
Their birthday,
An anniversary,
The holiday season.

You start to choke up.
Silently let the tears fall.
Say a prayer to them and for them.
Live in that memory for a moment
And continue with your day.

Sometimes you tear up at the mention of their name.
Grief caught at the back of your throat
When you reminisce of them one day,
When you have to explain to someone new
That your loved one is no longer here,
That they watch over you.
Your personal guardian angel
Keeping you safe, always.

There are days you laugh,
Thinking of a happy memory.
Days that you reflect,
Thinking what they might say.
There are days you cry,
When the emptiness hits harder than expected.

In all these times,
You never forget.
You always remember,
For where there is love,
Grief lasts forever.

SMILE

You make me smile.
I grin from ear to ear
Or give a subtle smirk,
One that comes when I think of you.

When I think of the good times,
When I think of the laughs,
The dirty talk,
The sweet talk,
The nerdy talk,
The heart-to-heart talk,
The kind of talk that hits my soul,
Keeping me connected to you.

A smile that happens
When I re-read our messages,
Bringing back the feeling
Contained in those words.

Connecting to that memory
How I felt in that moment,
How your words filled me up,
Inspired me,
Made me chuckle,
Taught me something new,
Provided a different perspective.

Those feelings,
Those memories,
Warm me up
Till I fill with sunshine
And smile … again.

RISE

Rise like the royalty you are.
Hold your head high
And shoulders back,
Chest proud.

Carry your crown
With all the pride
And strength
Running in your veins.

Rise above the doubt,
The hatred,
The fear,
The anger.

Come forth into the world
As the force you are,
No shrinking violet
But a bright sunflower.

Rise and be loud!
Make your ancestors proud.
Be their wildest dream
And their brightest future.

TOO MUCH

They always said I was too much.
Too smart,
Too loud,
Even too pretty.

I take up too much space,
Eat too much,
Drink too much,
Indulge too much.

They said it was too much for them,
Made them uncomfortable,
Seeing me live
So unapologetically.

OPEN ROAD

There is nothing quite like
Driving on an open road.

I don't mean top down,
Wind in your hair.

I mean the quiet,
The clarity of conscience
That comes from driving
And feeling the road beneath.

For me it is freeing.
Not a menial task
Nor a source of frustration.
Instead is a place...

A place that clears your mind.
Its own kind of meditation,
Where thoughts run wild
And ideas can be free.

The world melts away.
The more miles I drive,
The freer my mind feels,
The more I remember.

The road,
The music,
Gifting me memories,
Relieving my stress.

The calming feeling
Overtaking my whole being.
And I push the pedal harder
To keep the feeling going.

CAN YOU FEEL THE TREES?

That new book smell,
Nothing like it.
The smell of paper and ink,
The buzz of something familiar
But also unexpected.

Cracking open your latest purchase,
You inhale deeply,
Taking in the scent.
Committing it to memory,
You plunge headfirst reading.

Hours go by
As you read cover to cover,
Absorbing each word.

But another feeling lingers
At the tip of your fingers;
The feel of its pages.

Like an electric current,
Something has sparked,
Stirred some life.

The words leaping out at you,
Coming alive in every way.
An outdated adage
Credited to one's imagination.

But what if it were something more?
What if the paper held the secret?
Now seemingly lifeless,
But once a living tree
Taking in CO_2,
Letting out oxygen.

What if the energy from that tree,
Once green and lush,
Retained a small piece of soul?

What if the words lived
Because the paper once did?

As you hold your book in hand,
The pages beneath your fingers,
Ask yourself,
Can you feel the trees?

NOT IN THE MOOD

For any of it;
The bullshit,
The drama,
The hate,
The gossip.

Not in the mood
For racist individuals,
Homophobic folks,
Misogynistic persons.

I'm not in the mood
To deal with closed minds.
Those with blinders on,
Seeing only through binoculars,
Trying to hold steadfast
To their narrow views.

I'm not in the mood.
Not anymore.

PAINTED SKY

Dots of clouds
Suspended in air.
Fluffy cotton balls
On a brilliant blue canvas.

Hanging still
In the beautiful midday,
Stretching above the road
And beyond the horizon.

Midday turns to dusk.
White clouds giving way,
Turned slightly gray.
The sunset behind ablaze with color.

Blue yielding to pink,
Pink bleeding to orange,
Orange welcoming midnight;
A blanket for the stars.

White stars shine above,
Pinpricks of light
Against the blue-black night,
Turned on for all to see.

Midnight surrenders to daylight,
Yawning and stretching
As it lightens the sky,
Bringing with it soft sunlight.

Sky turns to a pale blue.
That familiar morning hue
Welcoming the day warmly,
Ready to paint its canvas again.

DAY ONES

The ones who always have your back.
Who've seen you through each act.

A part of every life season.
There for you through it all,
No matter the rhyme or reason.
There to pick you up after every fall.

The ones that celebrate you.
Know you inside and out.
Help you do you.
Always ready to shout you out.

Never-wavering faith.
Never doubting your place.
Reminding you: you are great
To go forth at your own pace,
That you never have to wait,
That you can take up all the space.

UPSTAGED

The chorus dances to and fro
As the prima ballerina
Fluidly spins her dark dance;
Bringing painful memories forth,
Stealing the spotlight,
Relegating the chorus upstage.

As she continues to turn,
The chorus slowly glisses forward,
Taking over the prima's space,
To shine briefly joyous moments
Once buried beneath, never seeing light.

The prima pirouettes effortlessly,
Knocking back the chorus.
She spins furiously,
Distracting the audience.
The chorus, momentarily stunned,
Explodes forward like a force
To block the prima from view.

Beginning their slow dance,
Moving as one to the orchestra's violins.
A slow, beautiful adagio,
Reminding the audience
The grace and beauty of many as one.

Showcasing that the many,
Although prosaic, seemingly plain,
Create a beautiful mosaic
That will always outlast
A singular and bleak prima
Hell-bent to never be upstaged.

CONFIDENCE

To many, it is a cape,
A badge, or a medal;
Something to show off,
Saying, "Look, I've got it."

Often mistaken
Or confused with
Bravado,
Cockiness.

Confidence is not brash,
Not a medal or badge.

More like a blanket;
Wrapping you in security,
Providing love and safety,
Supporting you all the way.

It envelops every part of you,
Giving you all you need.
The assurance so necessary
To go forth in this world.

SCARS

Reminders of the past,
Healed with time
By helping hands
And soothed over.

Although healed and faded,
Their messages linger.

Some are warnings
To never venture there again.

Some are joyous reminders
To live life to the fullest.

But the scars we cannot see,
Those made on our soul,

Hold the deepest tale
Of them all.

A billboard shouting,
"You have survived it all!"

BLUE SKIES

The telltale golden globe above.
Not a cloud in the sky,
Its presence a sign of joy,
Shining down endlessly.

Not a single cloud present
To steal the sun's splendor.
A blue sheet stretched above.
Calm spreading as vast as its reach.

Golden rays providing warmth,
Filling each cell, head to toe.
Nothing but blue skies
Smiling at me.

ADAPTING

Like the great forests
Of North America
Who must shed their leaves
Before winter's cold—
Retaining their strength
To survive the coming cold.

So, too, must you
Retain your strength
Through the winter of life,
Remembering to adapt
As life's seasons change
And test your every limit.

For if you do not,
You will break and fracture
Like a great oak
Rather than bending
With each and every test
As bamboo can only do.

LOOK AROUND

Look around
This world
You inhabit
Each day.

Its marvels
Everywhere
To be seen,
To be heard.

It is not on a screen
Nor through a VR set;
It is all around,
Above and below.

Even these pages
Can never replicate
The utter experience
That is living life.

Look up from the devices;
Put them face down.
Go out into nature;
Breathe the fresh air.

Printed in the United States
by Baker & Taylor Publisher Services